FASHION DESIGN DRAWING

FASHION DESIGN DRAWING

Patrick John Ireland

A HALSTED PRESS BOOK

JOHN WILEY & SONS
New York

© Patrick John Ireland 1972
First published 1972
Second edition 1975

Printed in Great Britain
Published in the USA by
Halsted Press, a Division of
John Wiley & Sons Inc, New York

ISBN 0 470 42837 6
Library of Congress Catalog Card No. 73-134681

CONTENTS

INTRODUCTION

The purpose of this book is to help design students and people in industry to develop fashion sketching techniques. It is most important to understand what the term fashion sketching means. I have grouped four styles of drawing under the following headings:

Design sketching: refer to pages 38–47

Production sketching: refer to pages 48–59

Presentation drawing: refer to pages 60–73

Fashion illustration: Fashion illustrating is promoting designs which are already complete. The fashion illustrator would not design but illustrate clothes for promotion and he would work for magazines, newspapers, poster designs, books etc.

It will be noticed that details reappear in various chapters to remind the reader of their importance. It will be seen that I have provided a number of specimen drawings to help the reader to understand the various techniques and their purposes. Fashion trends constantly change and it should be noticed that factors such as political and social events bring about changes to the fashion scene. The current trends are most versatile and offer different looks i.e. the gipsy look, the maxi and mini looks, the Indian look etc. For this reason I have purposely inserted a section at the end, illustrating a varied selection of current looks and techniques.

FASHION FIGURE PROPORTIONS

The vertical or balance line in the figure poses must be drawn from the pit of the neck to the supporting foot to indicate that the head and neck are above the supporting foot.

It is always useful to draw this line very lightly when starting your sketch (see pages 14–17).

When sketching, you should remember that the fashion figure is eight heads tall.

The beginner should always draw the nude figure first with very light pencil lines and check the position of bust, waist, hips and overall proportions. In this way the lines will not show in your finished work. When sketching the garment you will find it most helpful to draw lightly a line following the contour centre of the body (see page 17). This will serve as a guide when designing and placing relative details (see page 19). You will improve your skill by practising drawing from a model or from fashion photographs. It is necessary for the designer to be able to draw the figure. It would be, therefore, advantageous to attend life drawing classes and to make a study of anatomy. However, if this is not possible you can learn to sketch the figure and achieve successful results by following the illustrated methods.

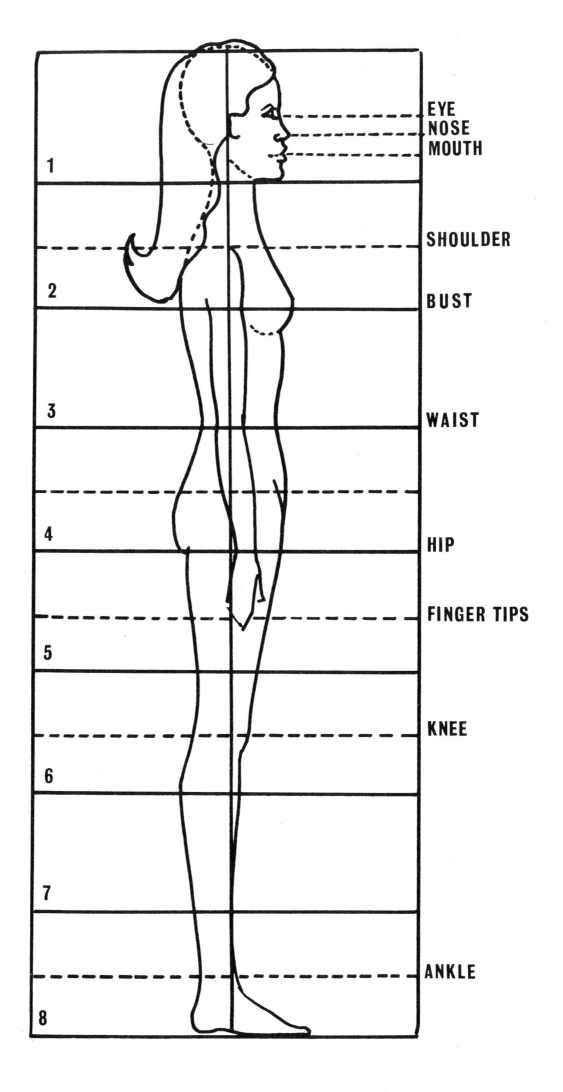

EYE
NOSE
MOUTH

1

SHOULDER

2

BUST

3

WAIST

4

HIP

FINGER TIPS

5

KNEE

6

7

ANKLE

8

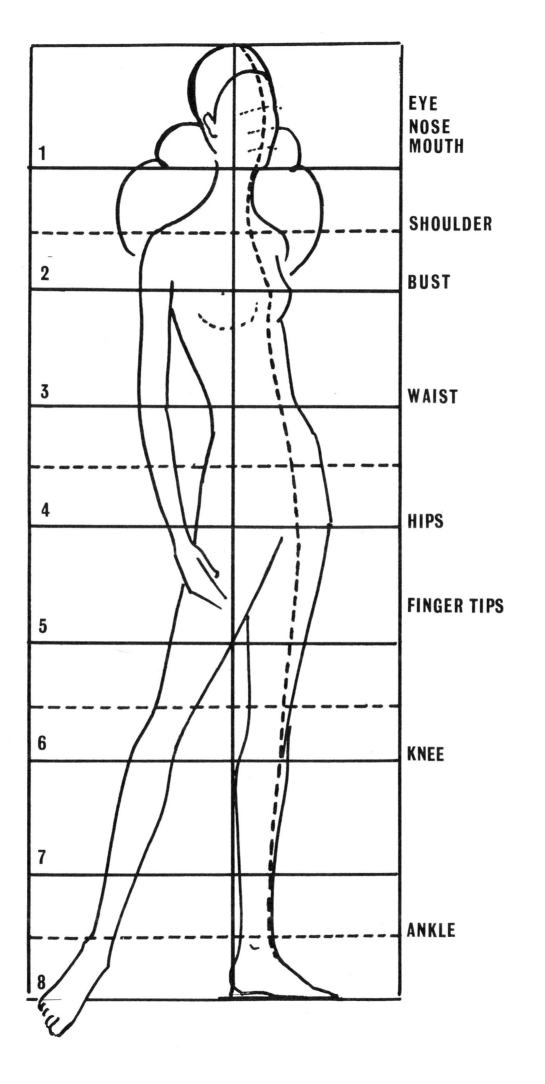

EYE
NOSE
MOUTH

1

SHOULDER

2
BUST

3
WAIST

4
HIPS

FINGER TIPS

5

6
KNEE

7

ANKLE

8

9

This sketch gives an outline of the average proportions of the female figure. It helps to calculate the height of the figure by the number of heads in the body. In the average woman the head will divide into the height about $7\frac{1}{2}$ times. For fashion drawing the number is increased to $8–8\frac{1}{2}$ times.

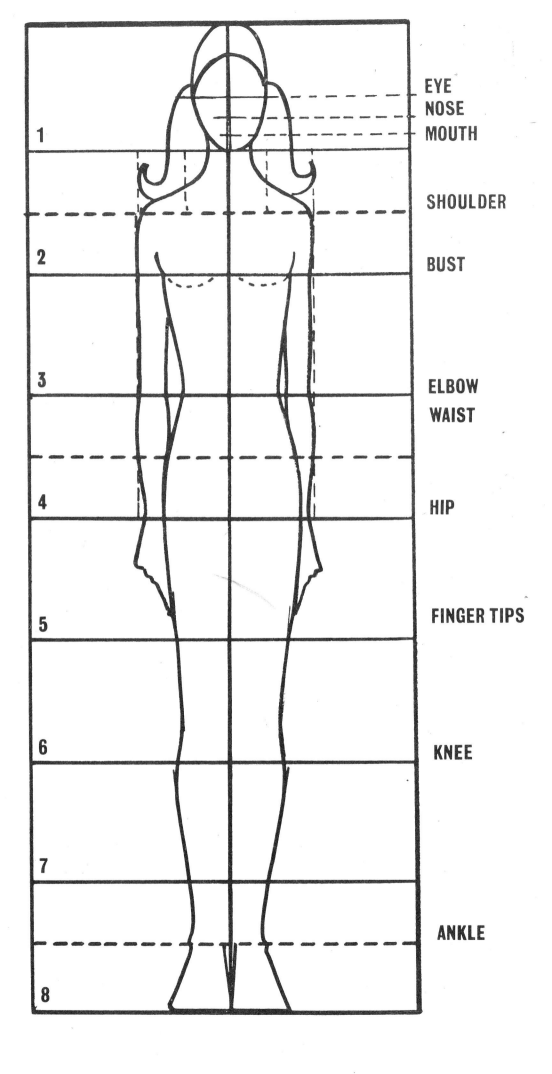

EYE
NOSE
MOUTH

SHOULDER

BUST

ELBOW

WAIST

HIP

FINGER TIPS

KNEE

ANKLE

1
2
3
4
5
6
7
8

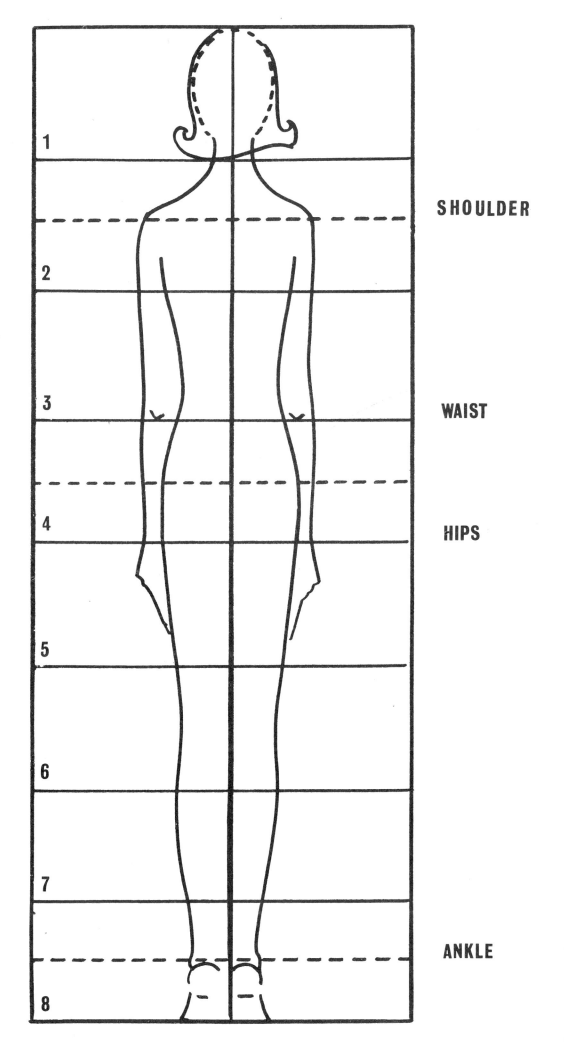

1

SHOULDER

2

3

WAIST

4

HIPS

5

6

7

ANKLE

8

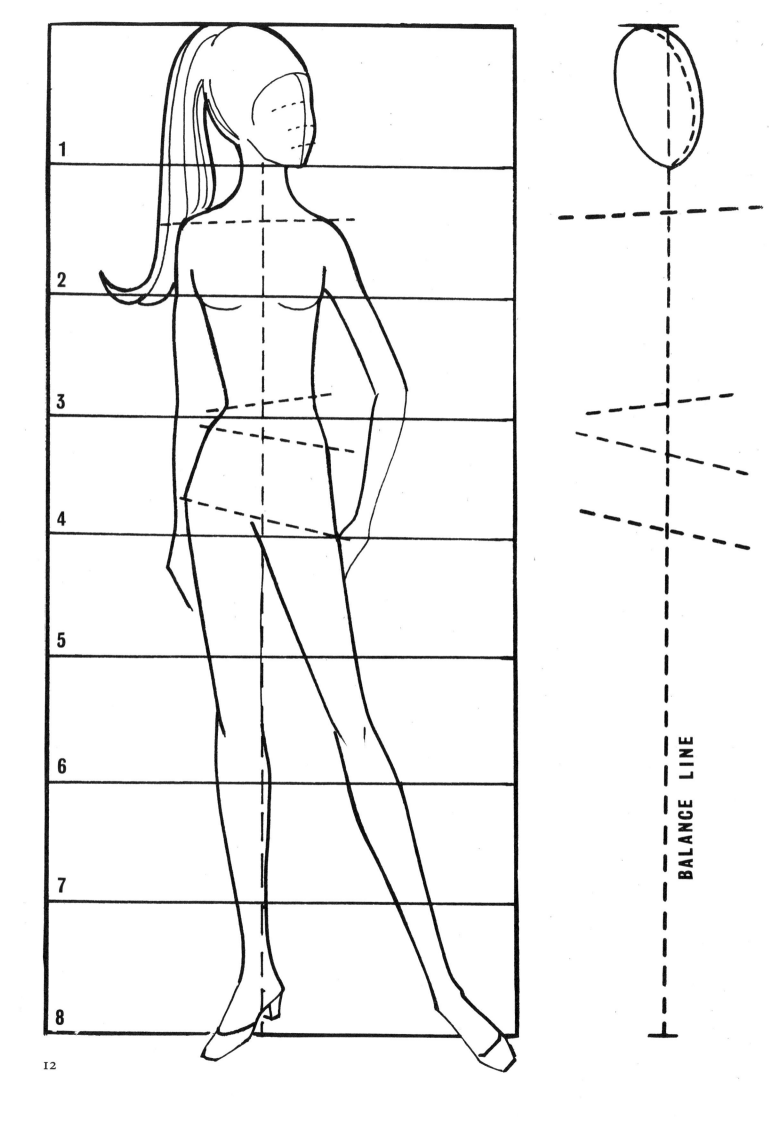

1

2

3

4

5

6

7

8

BALANCE LINE

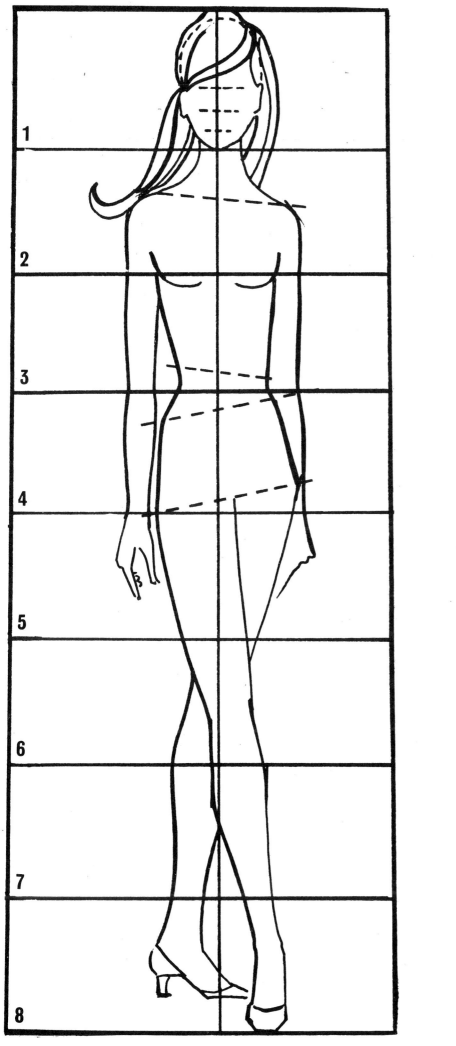

1

2

3

4

5

6

7

8

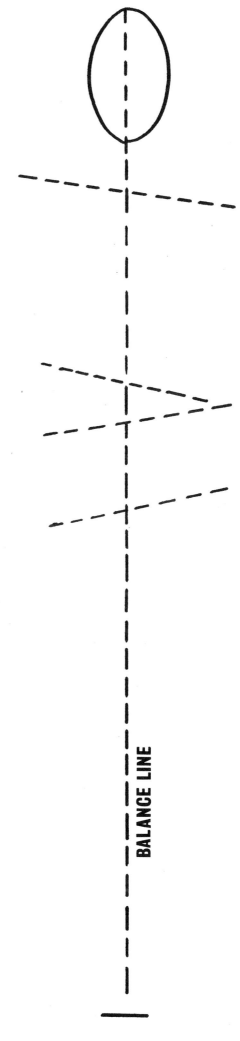

BALANCE LINE

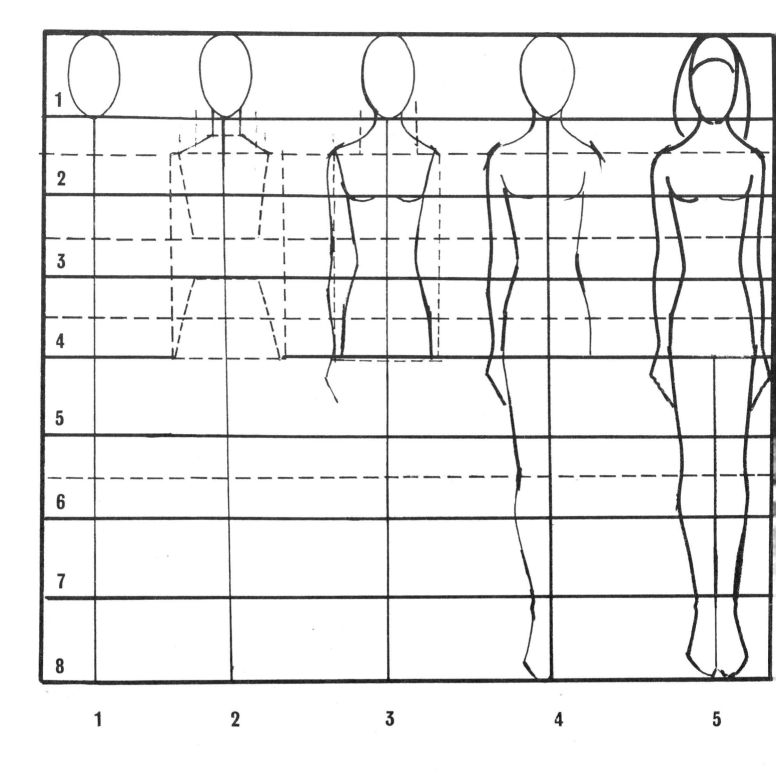

As an exercise work out the figure proportions as above, using the lines as a guide.
Practise this several times, then try to sketch the figure without the aid of the
lines.

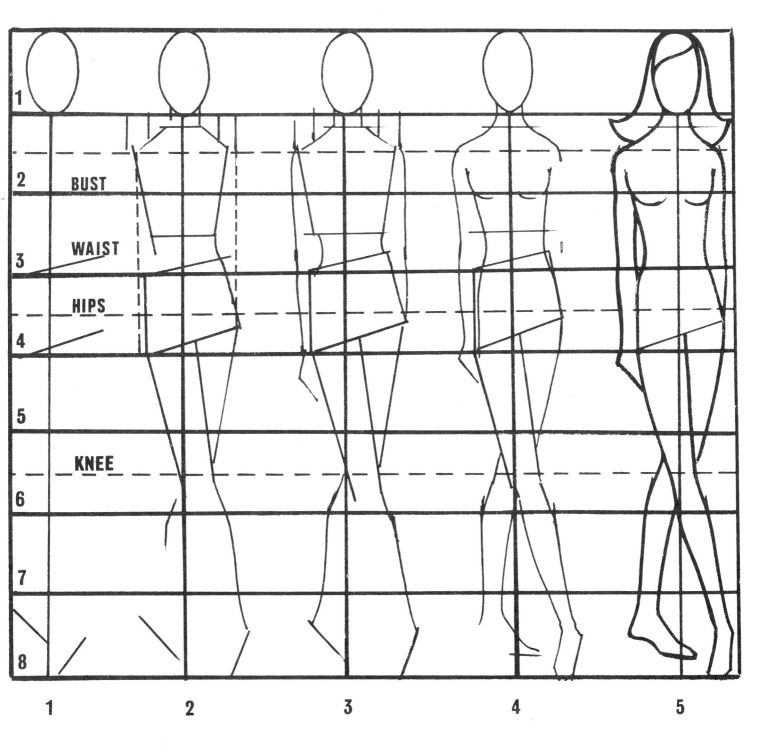

A variation of the pose with the weight on the left leg. Work from diagram, then try sketching the pose freehand. At this stage you need not worry about details. Simply sketch the outline, noting the proportion of the figure.

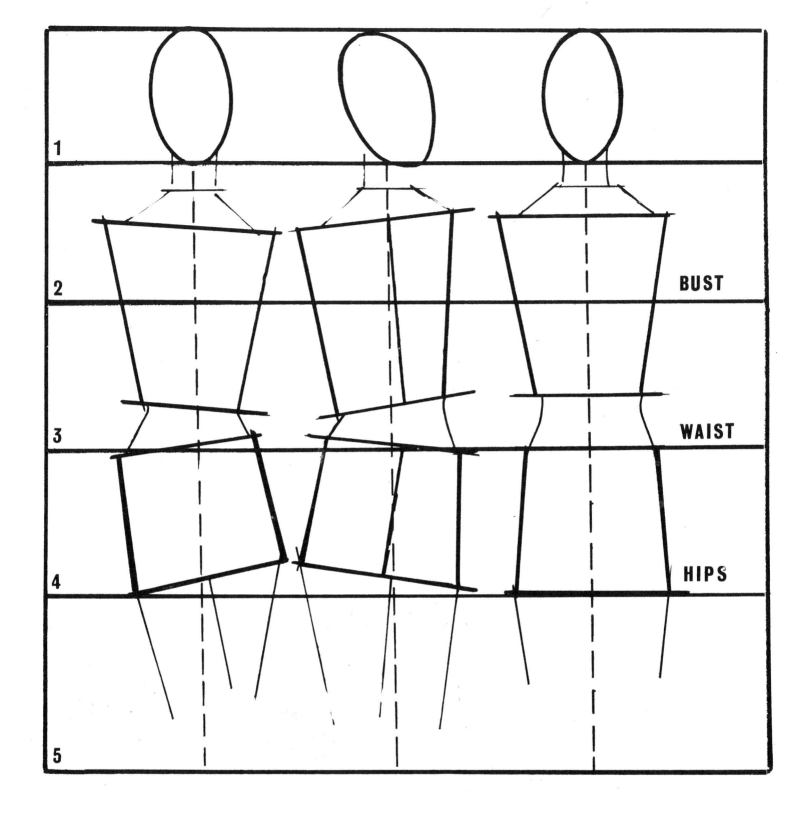

These diagrams show various degrees of torso tilt depending upon how much of the body weight is being carried by the supporting leg. A shoulder or hip may be dropped or raised to express more action in your sketch.

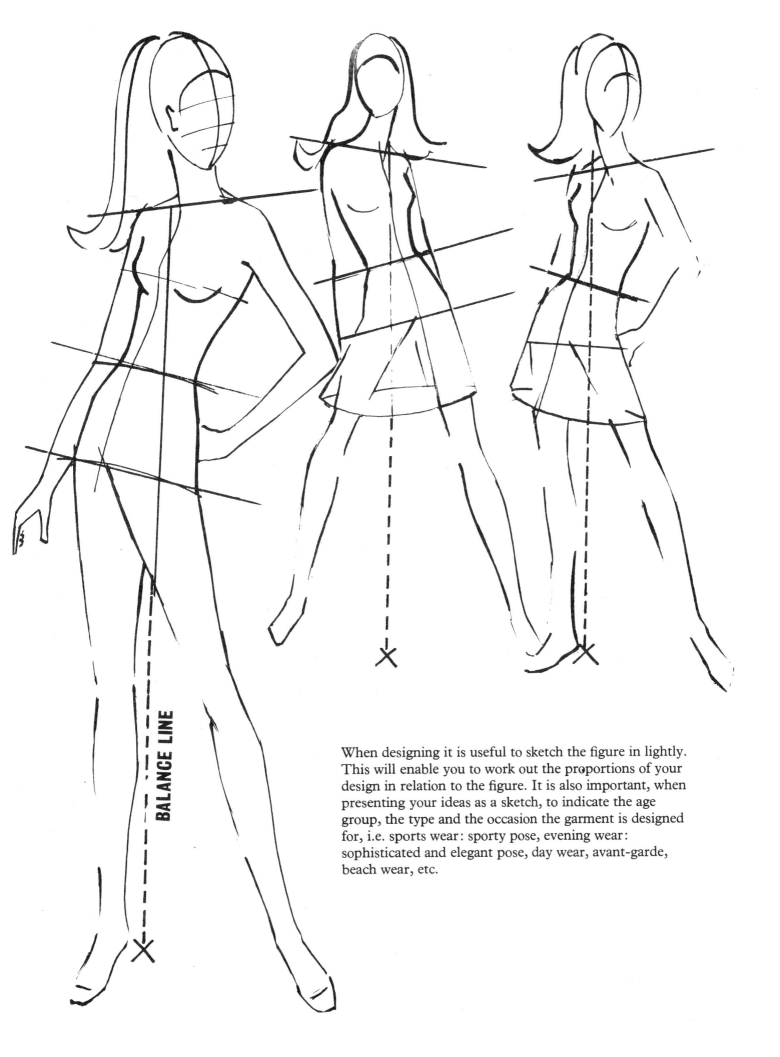

BALANCE LINE

When designing it is useful to sketch the figure in lightly. This will enable you to work out the proportions of your design in relation to the figure. It is also important, when presenting your ideas as a sketch, to indicate the age group, the type and the occasion the garment is designed for, i.e. sports wear: sporty pose, evening wear: sophisticated and elegant pose, day wear, avant-garde, beach wear, etc.

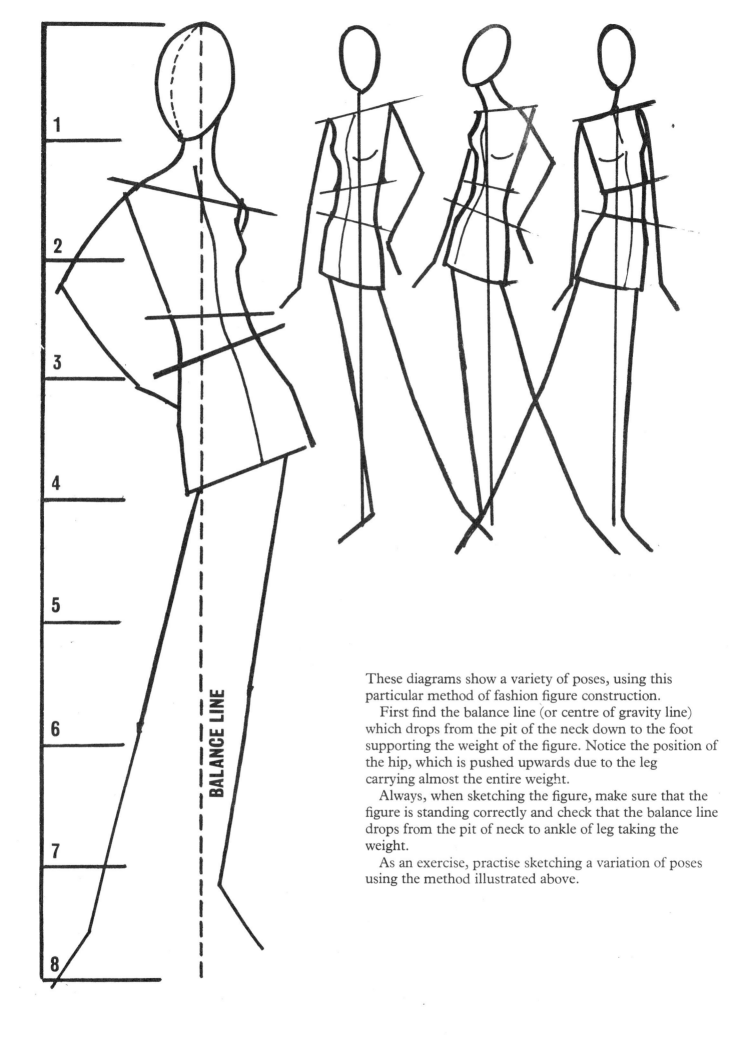

These diagrams show a variety of poses, using this particular method of fashion figure construction.

First find the balance line (or centre of gravity line) which drops from the pit of the neck down to the foot supporting the weight of the figure. Notice the position of the hip, which is pushed upwards due to the leg carrying almost the entire weight.

Always, when sketching the figure, make sure that the figure is standing correctly and check that the balance line drops from the pit of neck to ankle of leg taking the weight.

As an exercise, practise sketching a variation of poses using the method illustrated above.

1

2

3

4

5

6

7

8

BALANCE LINE

SHOULDER

BUST

WAIST

This is to show how the method can be adapted
when producing a fashion sketch.

Drawing arms

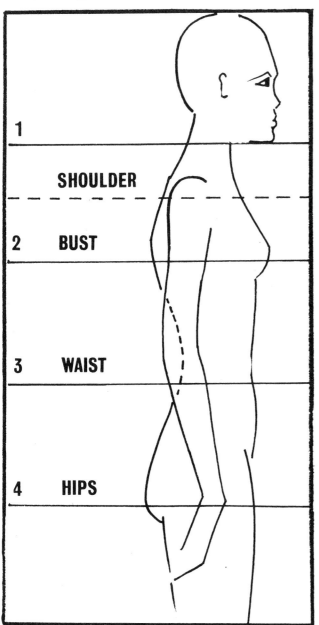

1

SHOULDER

2 **BUST**

3 **WAIST**

4 **HIPS**

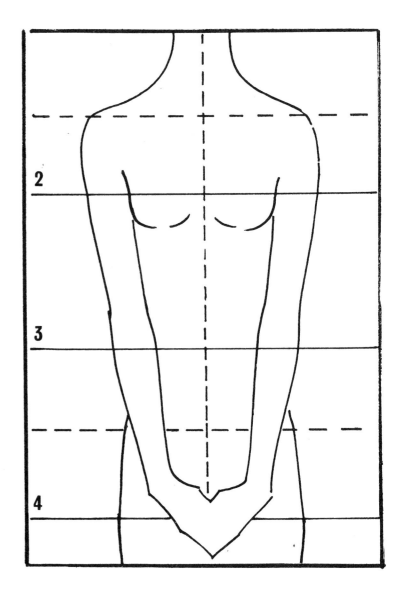

2

3

4

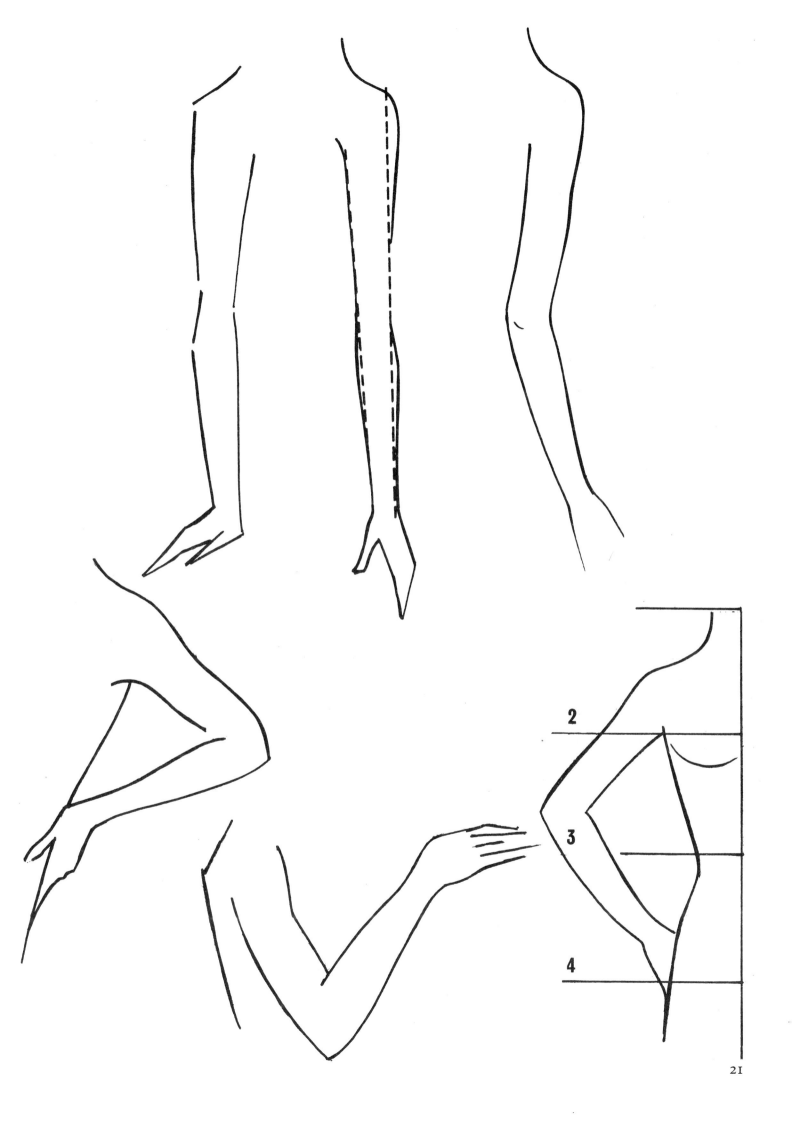

2

3

4

21

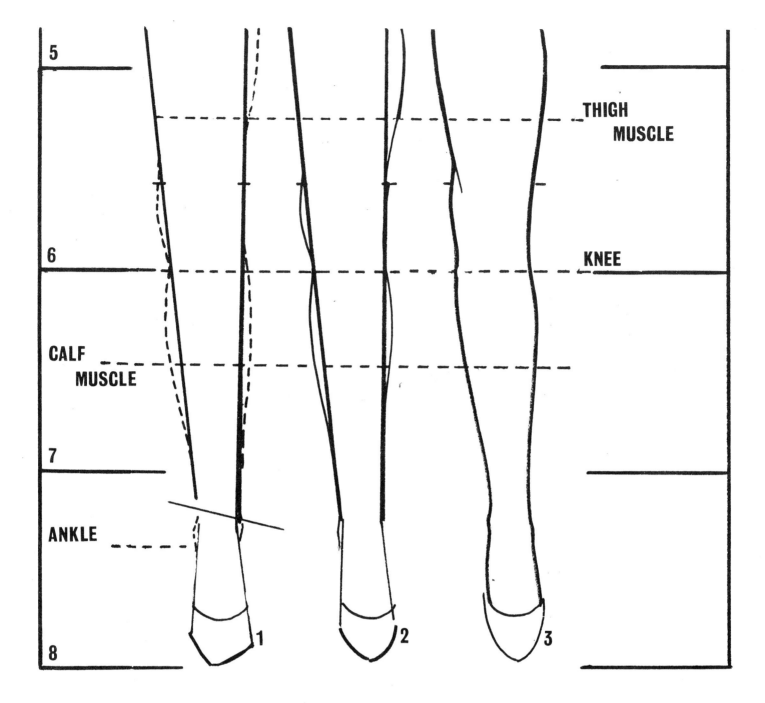

Drawing legs

Only a few lines are required when sketching the leg. Make sure that your sketch suggests the muscles of the leg to achieve the correct effect. Notice that the above diagrams indicate the principal muscles in the correct position. When fashion sketching it is important not to over-exaggerate the proportions of the leg in relation to the rest of the figure. Exaggeration in fashion illustration for advertising is permissible, but as you are concerned with fashion-design, sketching you should avoid extreme proportions as this can affect the balance of your design.

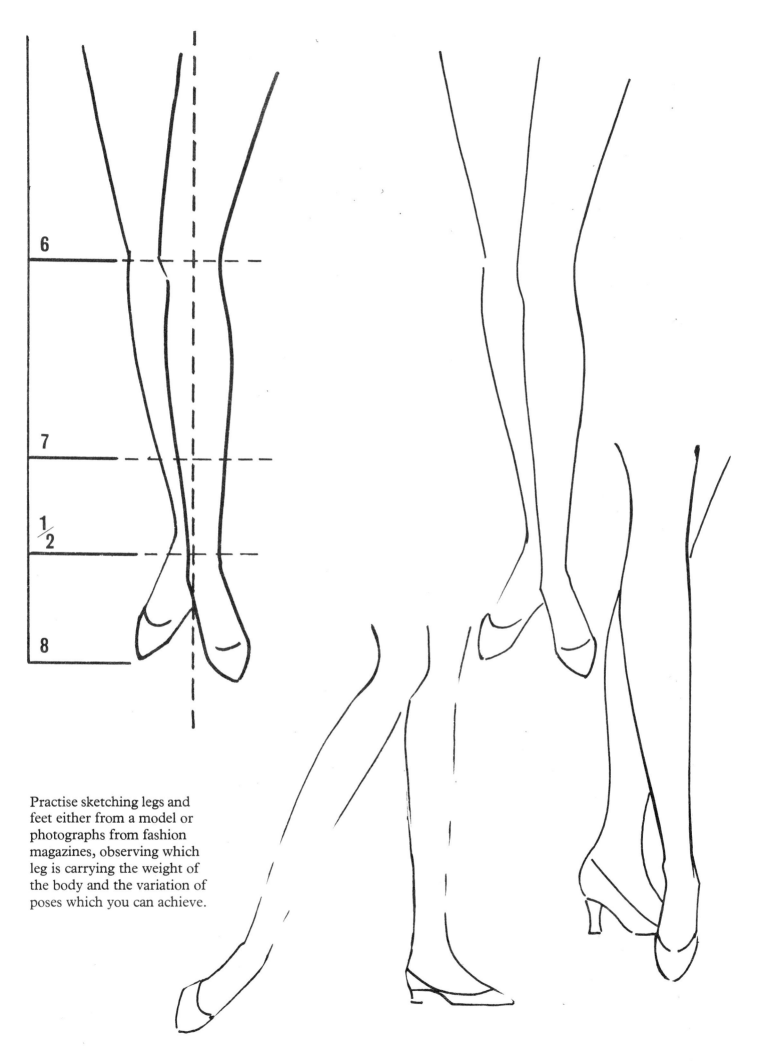

Practise sketching legs and feet either from a model or photographs from fashion magazines, observing which leg is carrying the weight of the body and the variation of poses which you can achieve.

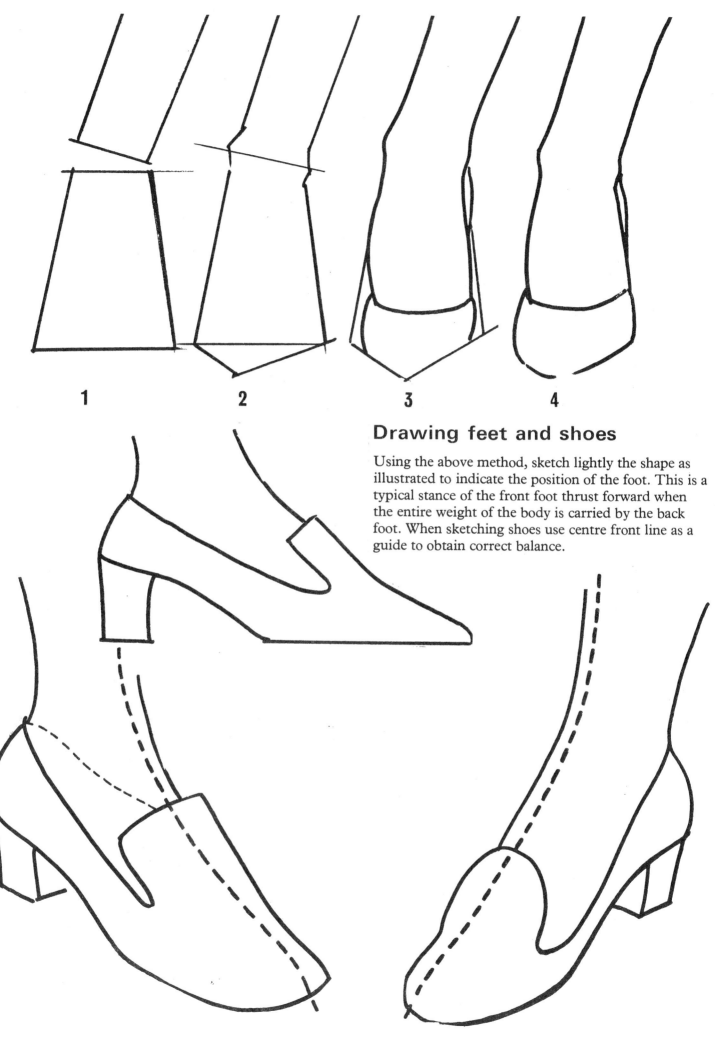

1   **2**   **3**   **4**

Drawing feet and shoes

Using the above method, sketch lightly the shape as illustrated to indicate the position of the foot. This is a typical stance of the front foot thrust forward when the entire weight of the body is carried by the back foot. When sketching shoes use centre front line as a guide to obtain correct balance.

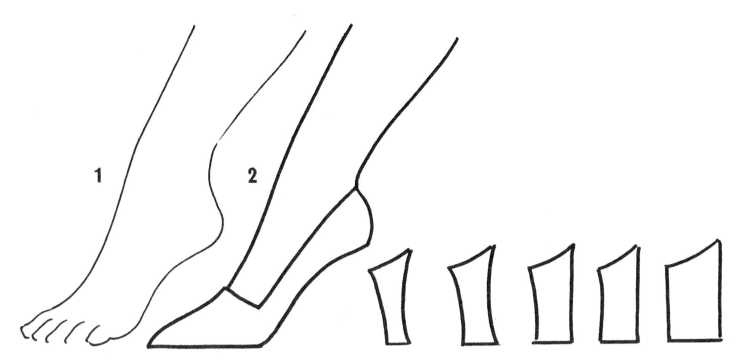

When sketching shoes draw lightly the shape of the foot first before you indicate the shoe itself.

As an exercise sketch shoes from different angles. Always remember to work from the centre front line, as indicated by dots.

HEADS, HAIRSTYLES AND HATS

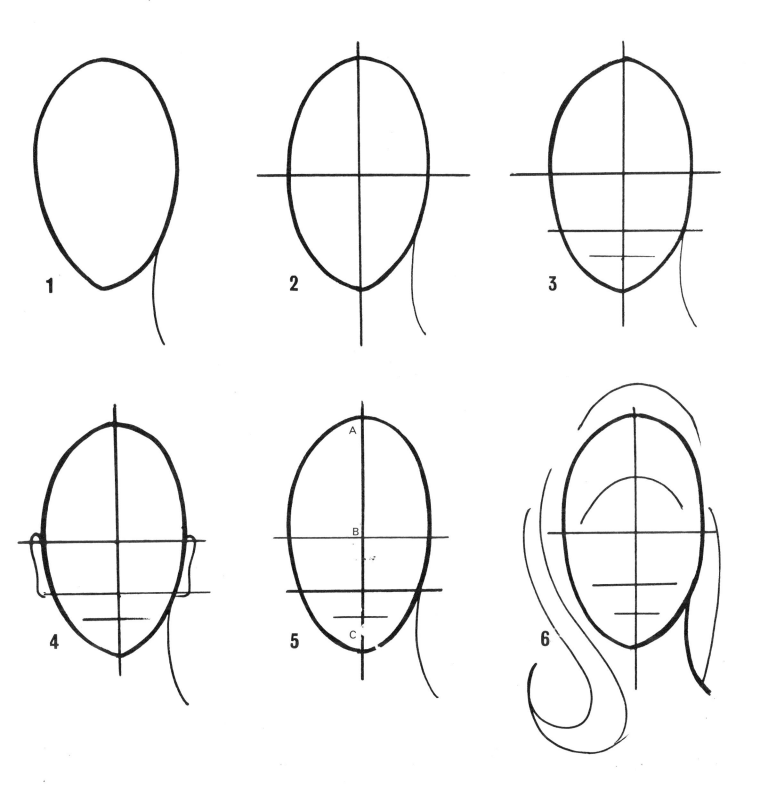

Drawing heads

1   The average head shape
2   Dividing the head into halves
3   Dividing the lower part into two, indicating nose and mouth
4   Position of the ears
5   Looking directly at the face; make sure that distance between a, b and c is identical
6   Completion of head, suggesting hair-line

In these illustrations the construction of heads
and hair-styles are shown by means of a few lines.

When sketching features, always remember that various effects can be obtained by drawing a few lines to achieve the different looks you wish to express. It is important to indicate age, type or fashion look.

Practise the various techniques of drawing eyes, nose, etc. as illustrated, then develop some methods of your own. As fashion trends change in looks and make-up, observe in journals and magazines the new look in the shape of eyebrows, eyelashes, lips, etc.

Drawing hairstyles

When designing and creating different looks, you will suggest a hair-style which will not only be complementary to the design but which will suit the style of the garment and the occasion for which the model has been designed. It is important, therefore, that a designer should be aware of new looks in hair-styles as fashions are constantly changing. Keep in tune with the new trends by studying fashion magazines, hair-dressing journals, posters, TV films, newspaper articles, fashion shows, etc. Your sketches need only suggest a style by the use of a few simple lines which must be carefully selected. On the following pages a variety of techniques are illustrated. You should work from some of these styles and then develop some of your own techniques.

PEN

BRUSH

PEN

BRUSH

FELT PEN

BRUSH

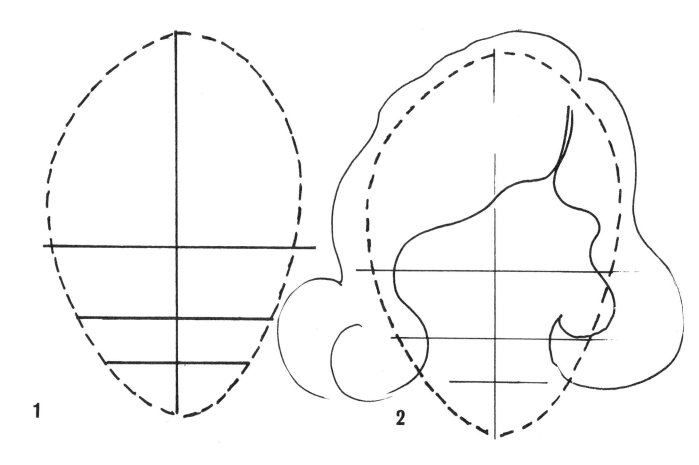

Here the development of head-construction is shown in five stages.

5

A number of techniques to suggest hair-styles.
A few lines can look most effective. It is unnecessary
to draw the hair in great detail.

Drawing hats

You should remember, when designing hats, that it is important to suggest the correct shape you wish to express with a few lines. Practise sketching different shapes of hats from a model working at various angles. If you are not working directly from a model, use a milliner's model or stand.

When designing hats make sure the hat is correctly positioned on the head. Draw with light pencil lines the shape of the head and then sketch your design, making sure the hat surrounds the head.

DESIGN SKETCHING

The purpose of design sketching is to develop ideas and to get them down as quickly as possible.

Design sketching is rather like handwriting. In both, you will be able to develop a style of your own.

The drawings should be clear without undue detail at this stage. Hands, legs and heads need only be suggested.

When sketching and developing an idea the designer is experimenting with shapes, lines, patterns and textures.

It is useful to practise the drawing of some of the basic fashion figures either sketching them freehand or working from the relative charts (see page 42). A variation of poses is useful to show different points of interest.

The design sheets are only for the designer's reference, not for presentation. Any notes or detail drawings of collars, sleeves, etc. can also be developed on this sheet (see page 39).

Let the ideas materialize, changing the silhouettes and varying the details. If you should not like the idea you are working on just leave it and start again. Don't cross it out: you may wish to develop the sketch later.

From this sheet you can select the designs you prefer.

When fashion sketching it is not necessary to draw in great detail faces, legs, arms, etc. A few lines are sufficient to indicate these details. However, it is important to place the centre front line correctly to maintain the correct balance of your design, the positioning of darts, seams, style lines, etc.

Notice that in the above illustration the balance line is indicated by the dotted line extending from the head to the foot and the centre front line is indicated by a a heavier line.

When producing design sketches and developing ideas, always lightly sketch the centre front line of your figure. This line will act as a guide to obtain the correct balance for pockets, darts, etc.

Try sketching the same garment at different angles. Work with a model or put your garment on a dress stand.

When designing and developing your ideas work freely, adapting your design in various ways.

44

Darts

The placing of darts must be done with great care.
Consider carefully the effect you wish to achieve before
indicating the dart position.

These two pages illustrate a technique which enables you to work on layout paper (detail paper), i.e. a transparent sheet placed over a figure-guide taken from the figure chart shown on page 50. This method is most useful for those students who are not yet completely confident in sketching the figure freehand.

Production sketching

The importance of a production sketch is that every detail in the design must be clearly drawn or described for production purposes.

The sketch is usually a flat drawing which must have everything in proportion. The pattern cutter needs a sketch from which a pattern can be cut.

Great care must be given to the clarity of the sketch, to the placing of the darts, pockets, buttons, seams, etc.

A working sketch is an analysis of the fashion sketch. The designer must consider the practical aspects of the design, that is how the collar is attached, the type of fastening and the placing of the darts. A back view of the design is also required.

When the design has an intricate detail this should be drawn separately.

Notes should be given with the sketch explaining details which cannot be expressed by the drawing, i.e. fastenings, linings, etc.

To save time or as an exercise place a thin sheet of paper over your figure-guide and re-trace the drawing (see pages 50–51). For this purpose you may use layout paper, bank paper, typewriting paper or detail paper. Your drawing would then be made from your original design sketch or sample garment.

This is an example of a production sheet as used in industry. It gives details of the garment costing, i.e. materials, trimmings, yardage, sample colour, lining, interlining, etc. Notice the two figures shown on the chart. These will be used for illustrating the garment and for making sure that every detail is accurate (i.e. placing of darts, seams, pockets, buttons, etc.).

RANGE STYLE NO. DESIGN NO.

	CODE	COMPOSITION	WIDTH	YARDAGE	SAMPLE COLOUR
MAIN MATERIAL					
CONTRAST MATERIAL					
LINING					
INTERLINING					

	DESCRIPTION	SUPPLIER	DESIGN NO	PRICE	PER YARD	ZIPS	BUTTON HOLES
OUTSIDE PROCESS							
OTHER TRIMMINGS							

	DESCRIPTION	QUANTITY WIDTH	SUPPLIER	DESIGN NO	LINE BUCKLE	PRICE
BELT						
BUTTONS						

NOTES

49

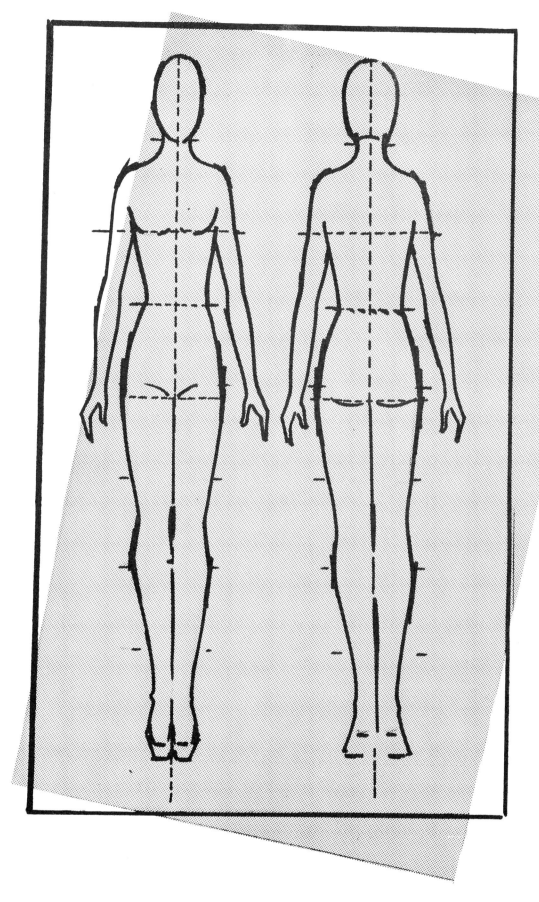

1   Cover the drawing of the figure with layout paper or a thin drawing
    paper.

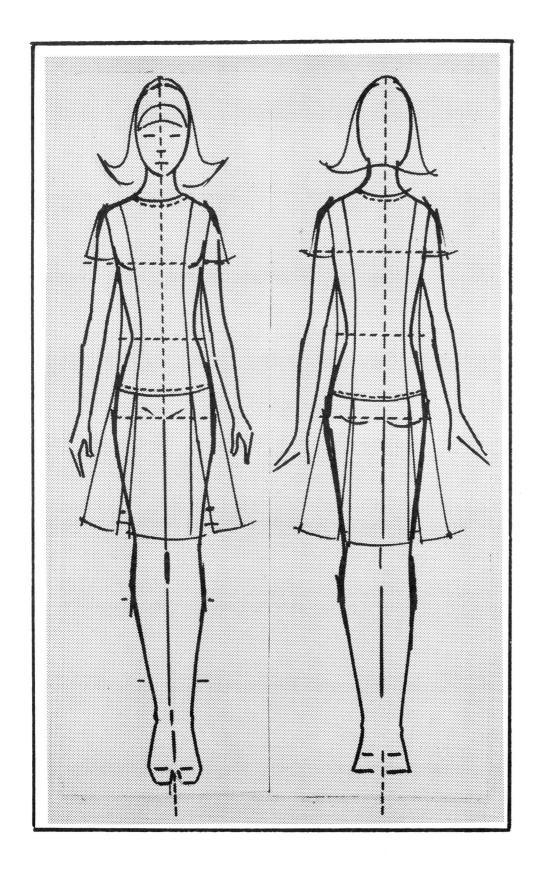

2 Sketch the design over the figures, placing the details with care.

3   Remove the paper from the figure-guide and complete the details of the design.

Sketch details of a design
i.e. tucks, sleeves, stitching, cuffs etc.

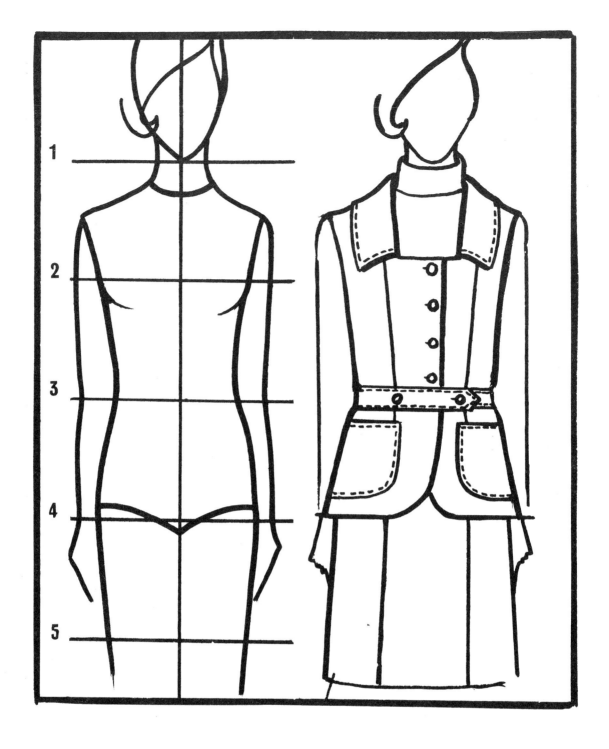

When making production sketches it is important to be aware of the figure proportions in relation to your design. Work over your figure-guide or draw freehand the basic figure shape using light lines which you can easily erase.

As an exercise, practise designing over the figure, creating different shapes and
lines, varying shoulder width, sleeve length, lapel shape, length of jacket, etc.

1   Straight double-breasted coat
    Button fastening
    Roll collar
    Raglan sleeve
    Pockets in panel seams

2   Slightly high-waisted coat
    Bias yoke and stand collar
    Kimono sleeve
    Four-button fastening
    Single-breasted

3   Double-breasted coat with
    four-button fastening
    Full-length set-in sleeve
    Belt attached to button on
    front fastening
    Revere collar

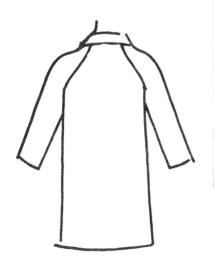

When designing notice how you can achieve various effects with the subtle use of lines and silhouettes: slightly raised waist above natural waist line, loose fitting line, straight, slightly flared or full skirts, variation of shoulder lines, etc.

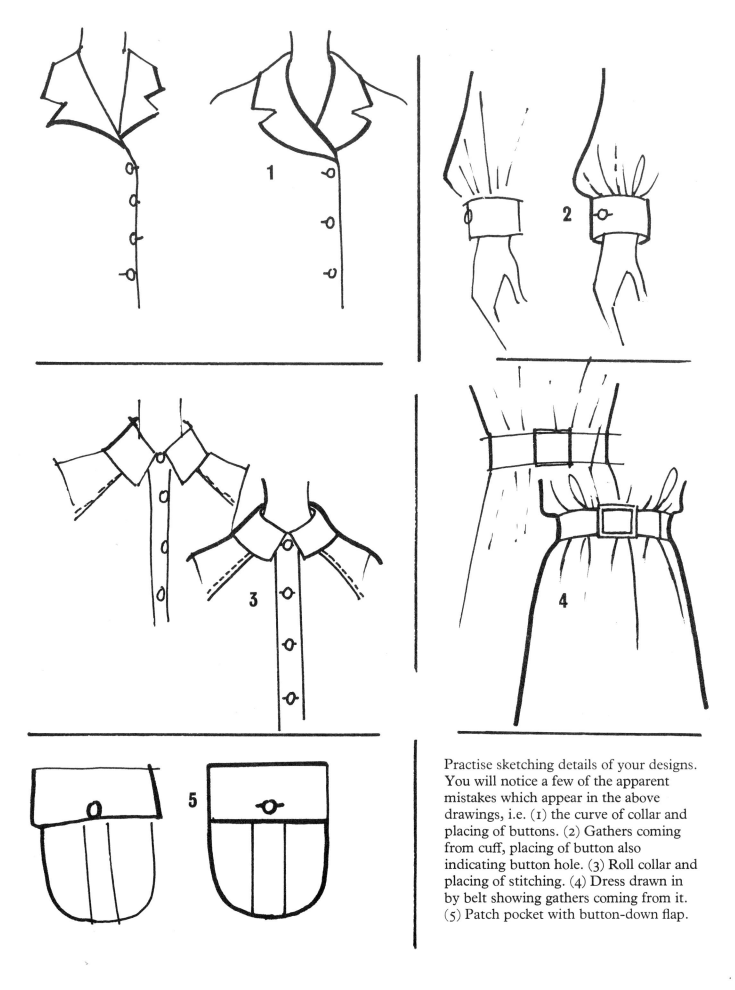

Practise sketching details of your designs. You will notice a few of the apparent mistakes which appear in the above drawings, i.e. (1) the curve of collar and placing of buttons. (2) Gathers coming from cuff, placing of button also indicating button hole. (3) Roll collar and placing of stitching. (4) Dress drawn in by belt showing gathers coming from it. (5) Patch pocket with button-down flap.

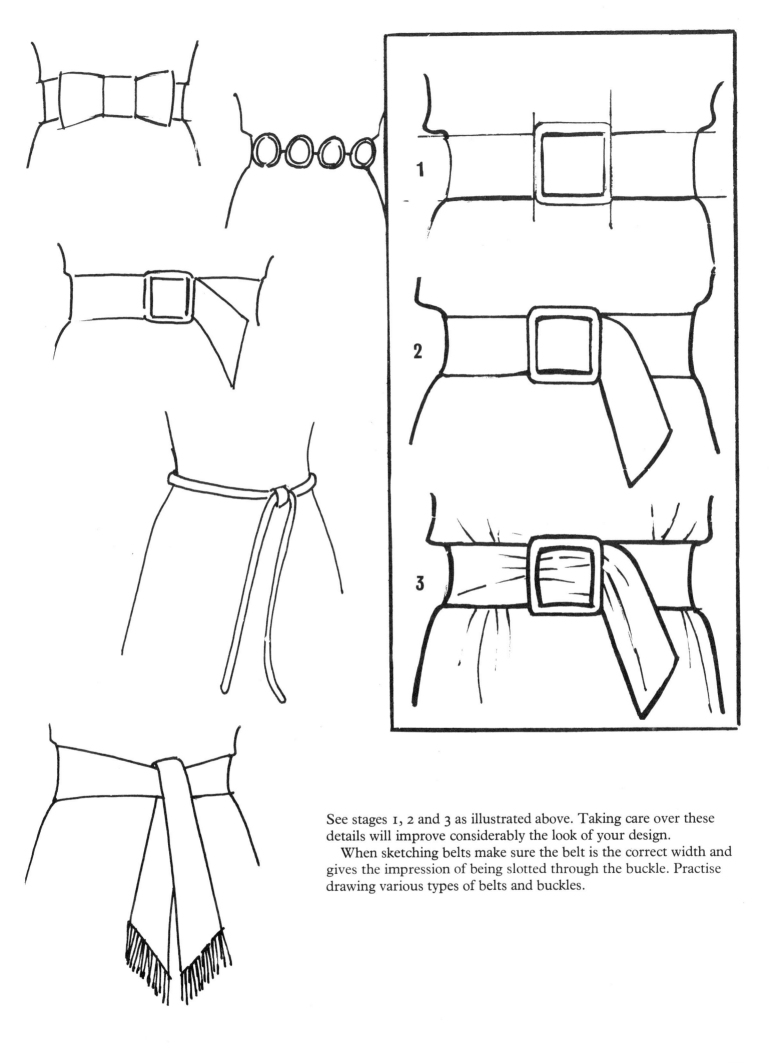

See stages 1, 2 and 3 as illustrated above. Taking care over these details will improve considerably the look of your design.

When sketching belts make sure the belt is the correct width and gives the impression of being slotted through the buckle. Practise drawing various types of belts and buckles.

Presentation drawing: layout of design work

Presentation is very important. When starting your presentation you should carefully consider the arrangement or 'layout' of your work. This will take very little time and will make a great difference to the look of your work.

Always allow a margin on your paper and proceed as follows: Place your design sketch with care on the sheet, then add the back view and notes giving the details of the garment, and attach a sample of material

to your sheet. Back views of garments can be drawn on a figure or can be shown flat (see page 66). The notes should clearly give all the necessary information. It is good practice to arrange your notes in a neat block. Fabric samples suggesting the material used for the garment should also be pinned or stuck to the sheet. These need only be small, no more than 1 in. Figures may be drawn to the hem line, or a full-length figure

may be presented. Should you work on a collection of drawings for either a client or a buyer it is advisable to keep to a standard size. This will make it easier for the client to look at your work.

It is advisable to keep your work in a folder. Never roll your sketches, particularly when you wish to show them, as this might spoil their appearance. An ideal size for working is 8×12 in.

This illustration shows the construction of the figure for a presentation sketch in
two stages:
1 Notice the use of centre front line. The balance line shows the correct
   distribution of weight on both legs.
2 Dress sketched round the figure balancing hem, neck line, sleeves, etc.

Striped cotton dress
1 Notice the balance
   line from point of neck
   to foot supporting the
   weight of the body.

1

2

Stripes drawn with care showing the use of the striped pattern in the design. This presentation sketch was made by using a fibre-tipped pen.

1   2   3

NOTES

_____
_____
_____
_____
_____

This page illustrates various ways of presenting the back view of a design: either on a figure or as a diagram.

1 2 3

Notice the three stages of drawing:

Notice guide line for collar, hem and centre front line ensuring balance.

1 The figure pose lightly drawn
2 Dress sketched round figure
3 Erase guide lines

The effect of this drawing has been obtained by using pen, ink and brush. Flower pattern voile is suggested with pen and ink on one side of the design; the hair is treated in sections. The pin tucks are drawn in with pen and ink. Notice the gathers coming from waist seam.

4 Presentation
Back view
Sample fabric and notes

1   2   3

Cotton Dress

Details: short set-in sleeves, patch
pockets from side seam, flat contrasting
collar, zip-back fastening.

1 Design carefully added round a figure which
   has been drawn with light lines.
2 Lines of figure erased, seams etc. placed with
   care.

3 Wash added with brush and black paint
indicating velvet, silk blouse with frills at
wrist (pen and ink). White paint applied for
seams and highlights at bend of arm, etc.

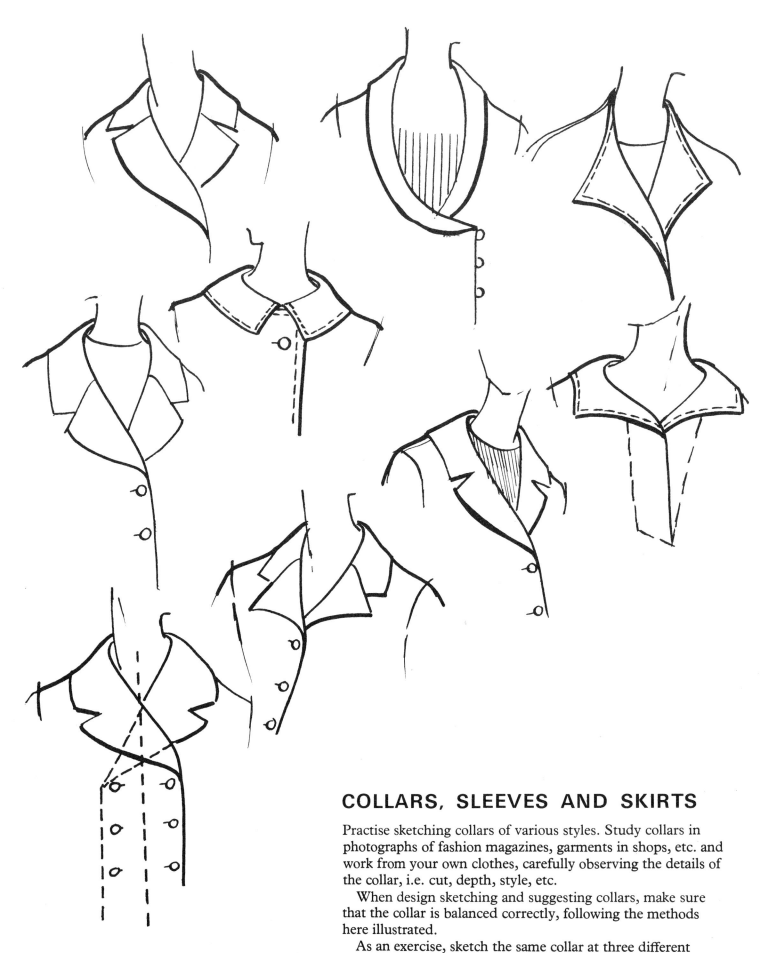

COLLARS, SLEEVES AND SKIRTS

Practise sketching collars of various styles. Study collars in photographs of fashion magazines, garments in shops, etc. and work from your own clothes, carefully observing the details of the collar, i.e. cut, depth, style, etc.

When design sketching and suggesting collars, make sure that the collar is balanced correctly, following the methods here illustrated.

As an exercise, sketch the same collar at three different angles.

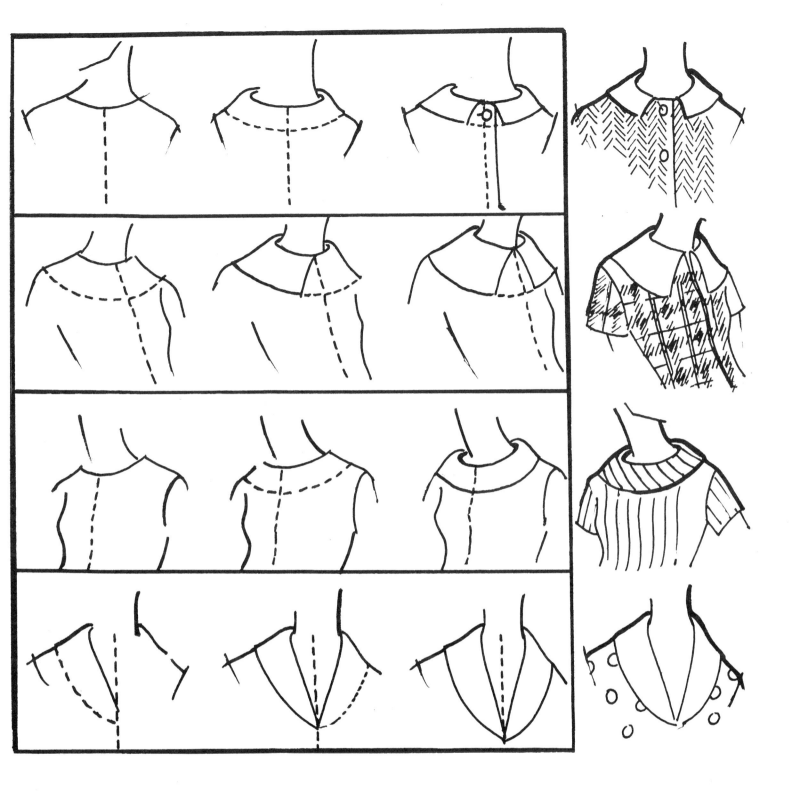

Sketch the following collars in the different stages as shown above, working from the centre front line for correct balance. Practise designing collars, sketching them at different angles.

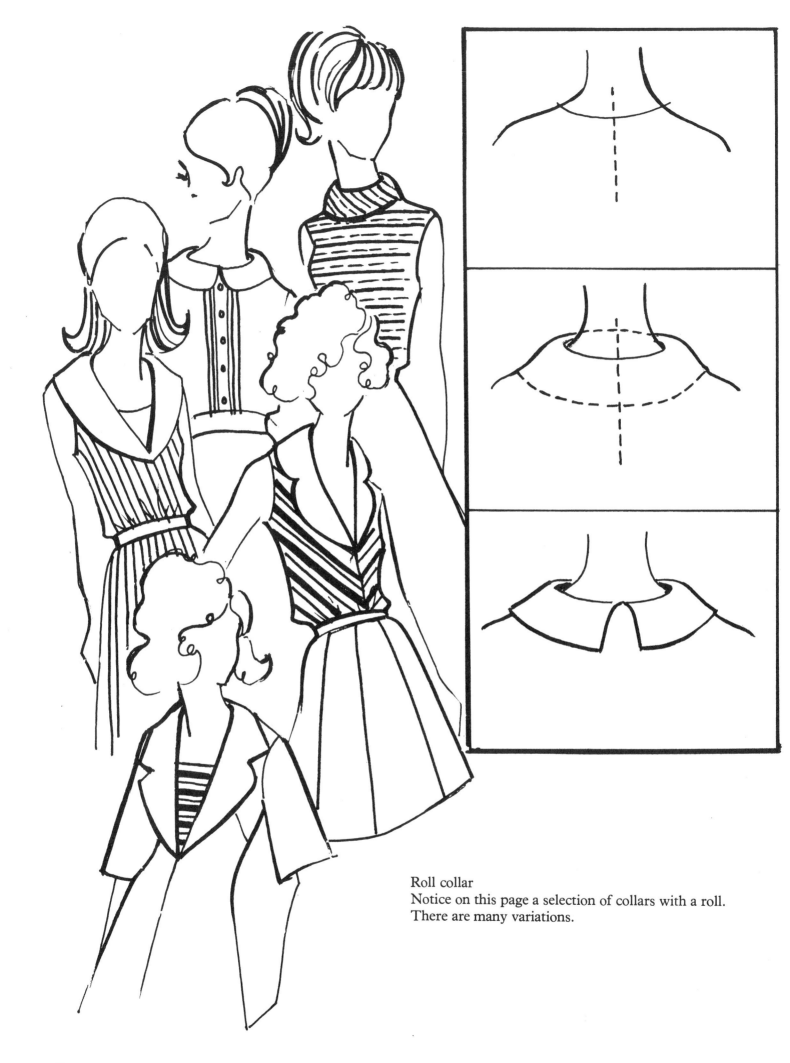

Roll collar
Notice on this page a selection of collars with a roll.
There are many variations.

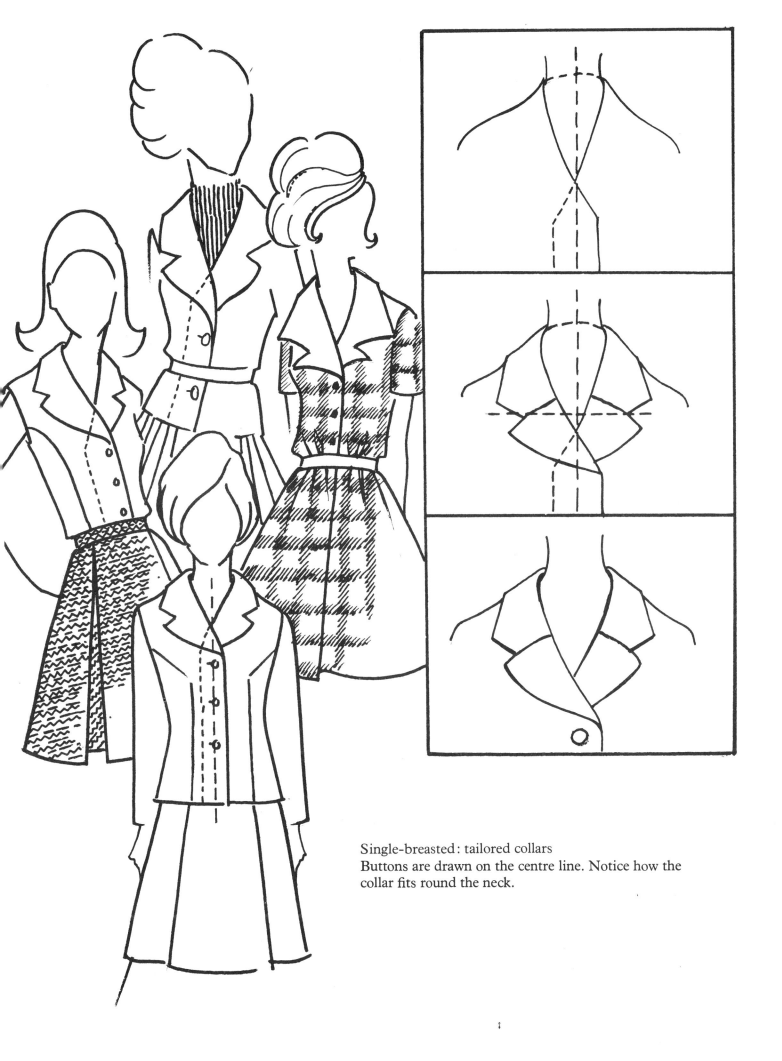

Single-breasted: tailored collars
Buttons are drawn on the centre line. Notice how the
collar fits round the neck.

Stand collar
Practise designing garments with
variations of stand collars. As a reminder,
the construction of head, and the use of
CF Line when balancing the design, have
been added.

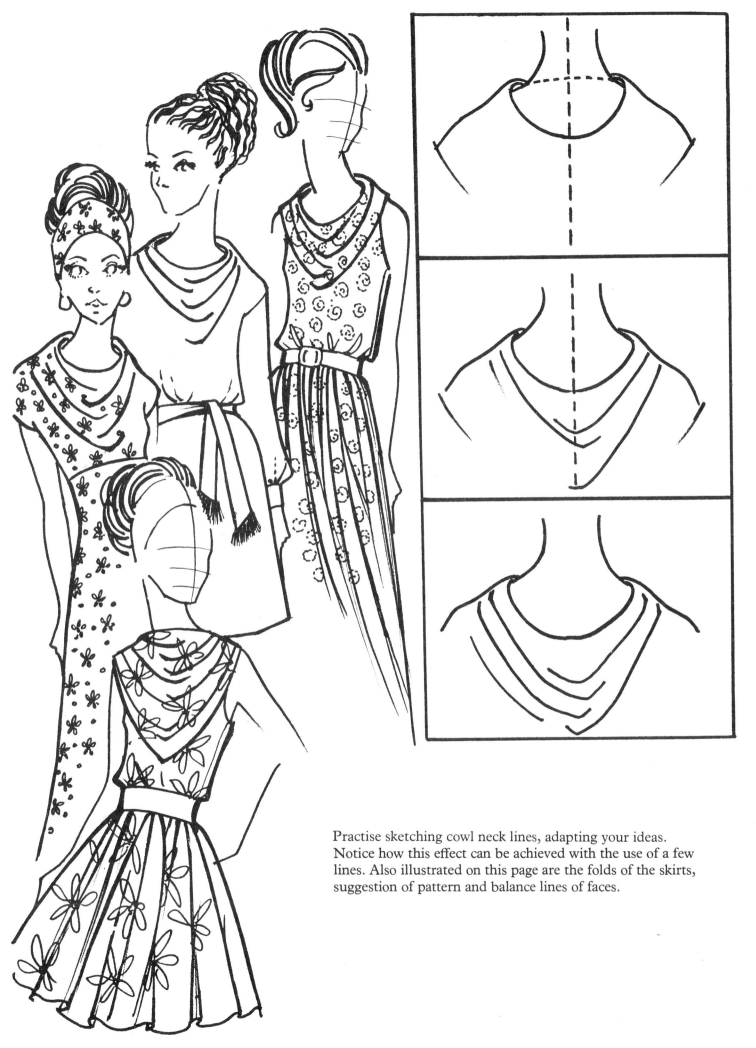

Practise sketching cowl neck lines, adapting your ideas.
Notice how this effect can be achieved with the use of a few
lines. Also illustrated on this page are the folds of the skirts,
suggestion of pattern and balance lines of faces.

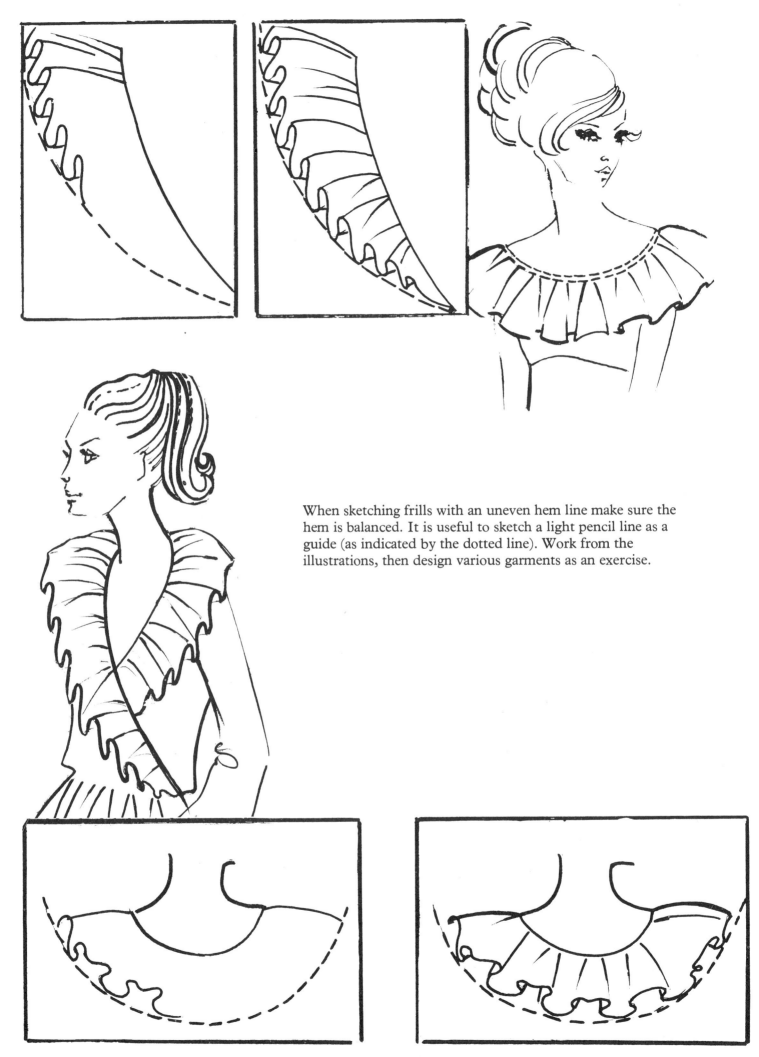

When sketching frills with an uneven hem line make sure the hem is balanced. It is useful to sketch a light pencil line as a guide (as indicated by the dotted line). Work from the illustrations, then design various garments as an exercise.

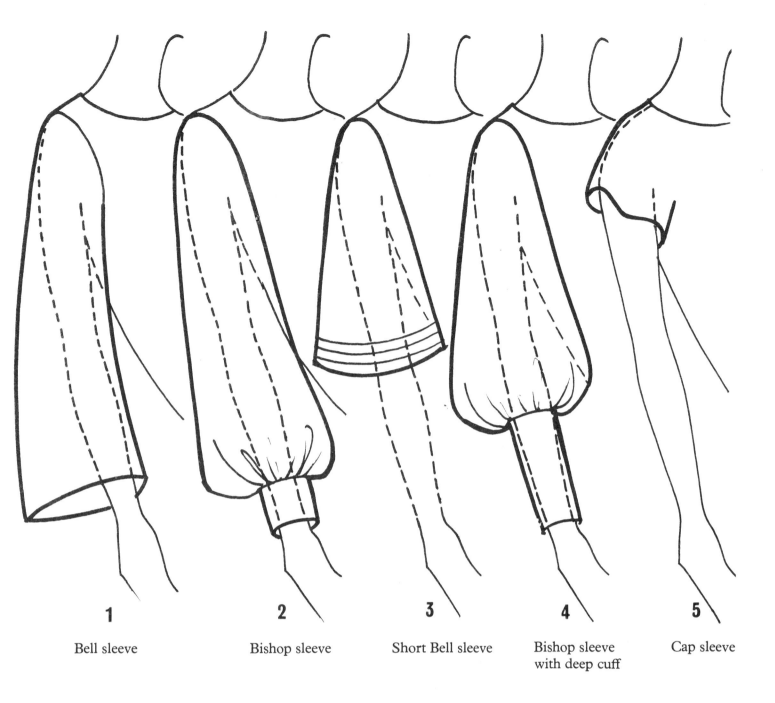

1 Bell sleeve

2 Bishop sleeve

3 Short Bell sleeve

4 Bishop sleeve with deep cuff

5 Cap sleeve

Drawing sleeves

When drawing the sleeve make sure that it surrounds the arm. Notice how folds appear at the elbow when the arm is bent in different positions. Practise sketching a variety of sleeves, varying your design and suggesting different materials to convey the feel and behaviour of the material in your sketch. It is a good exercise to sketch different sleeves, if possible, from a model; or ask a colleague to model for you. Observe the cut and the characteristics of a number of sleeves and express this idea by using as few lines as possible.

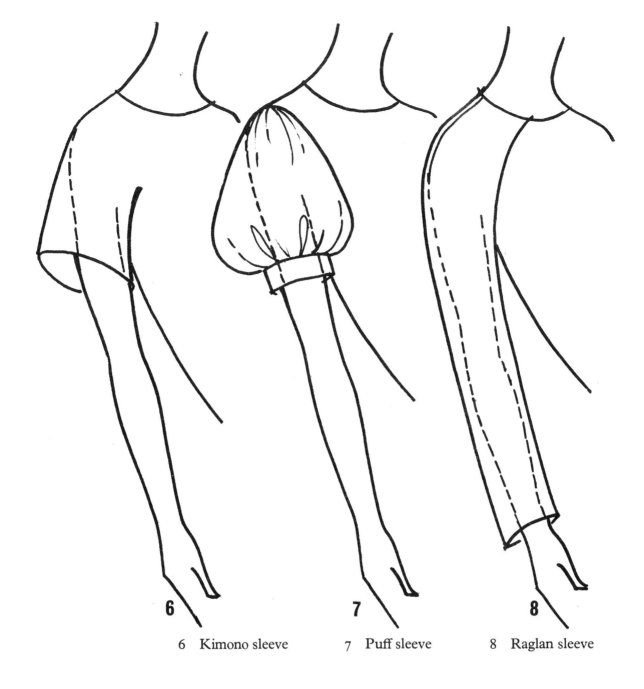

6   Kimono sleeve   7   Puff sleeve   8   Raglan sleeve

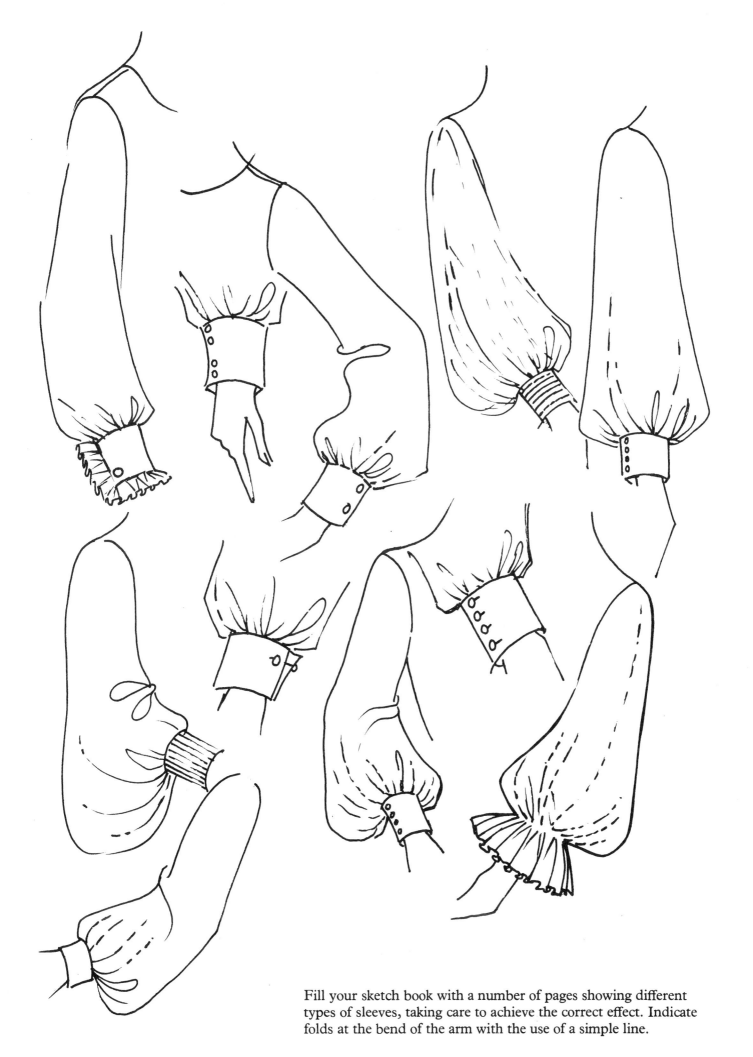

Fill your sketch book with a number of pages showing different types of sleeves, taking care to achieve the correct effect. Indicate folds at the bend of the arm with the use of a simple line.

Follow the three stages as illustrated above. Notice the hem line and the effect of soft folds. Practise sketching variations of this sleeve.

Drawing skirts

Practise sketching a variety of skirts in your sketch book. Design for different materials, suggesting the folds with the use of a few lines only. Take care, when drawing the hem line, to obtain the effect required.

Three basic skirt shapes:
1 Straight
2 Slightly flared
3 Circular

Note: dotted line indicates hip, CF line
and also hem line of skirts.

Notice weight on both feet

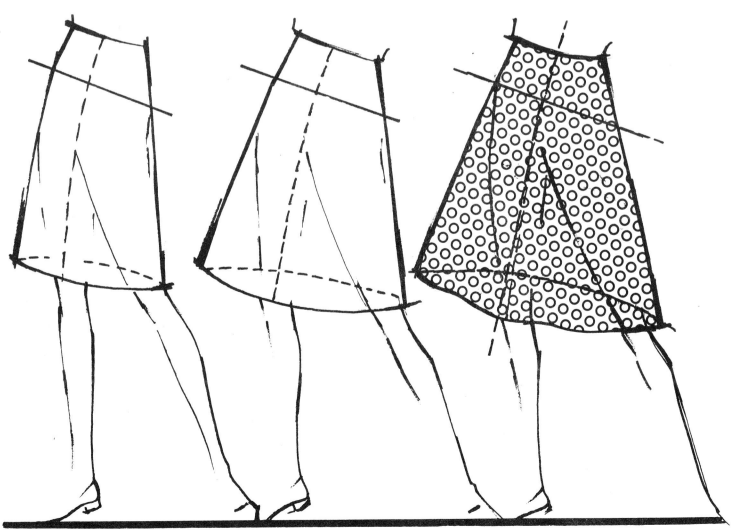

Notice weight on right foot

1   The mini skirt

2 and 3   Short skirts above the knee

4 Just below the knee   5 The midi skirt   6 Floor length

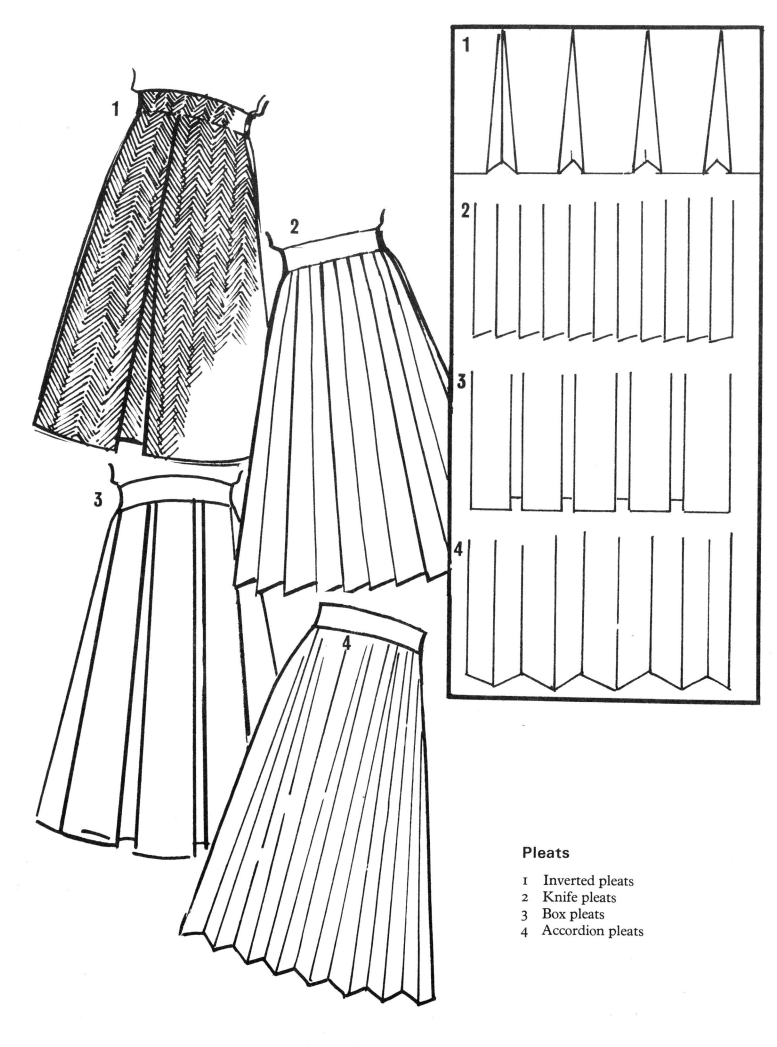

Pleats

1 Inverted pleats
2 Knife pleats
3 Box pleats
4 Accordion pleats

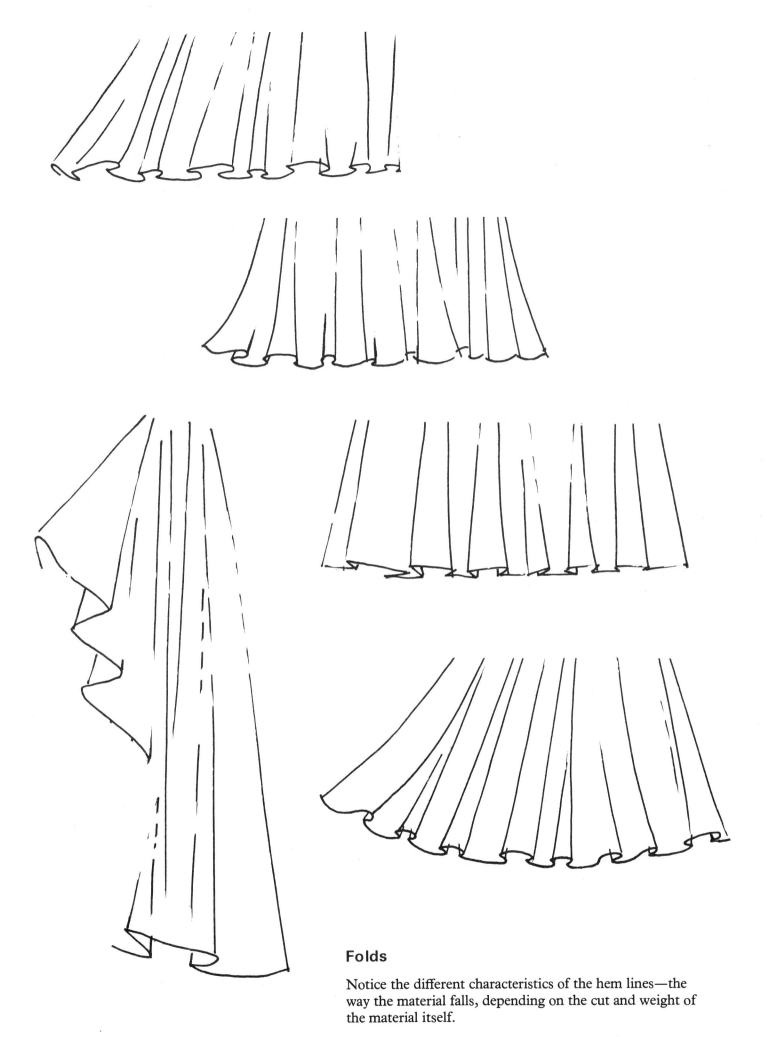

Folds

Notice the different characteristics of the hem lines—the way the material falls, depending on the cut and weight of the material itself.

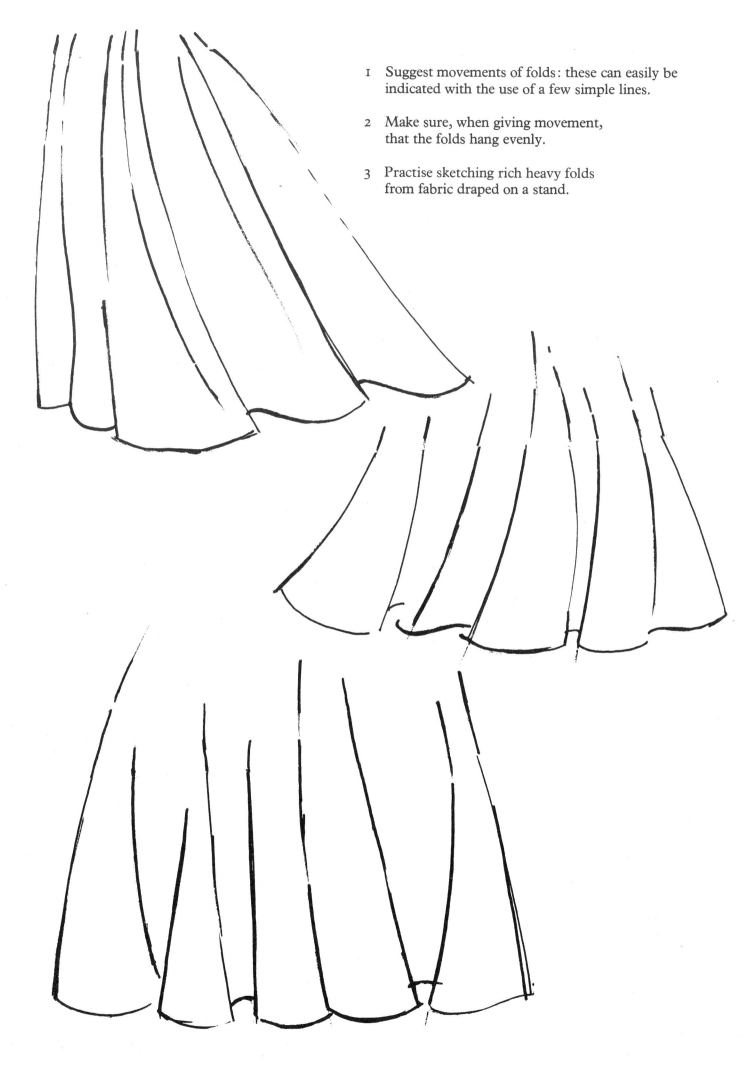

1 Suggest movements of folds: these can easily be indicated with the use of a few simple lines.

2 Make sure, when giving movement, that the folds hang evenly.

3 Practise sketching rich heavy folds from fabric draped on a stand.

FABRICS

Fabrics are an important source of inspiration for the designer. It is essential, when design sketching, to suggest textures, patterns and the behaviour of fabrics, i.e. how a fabric drapes and falls into folds, to indicate if the fabric is heavy, light or transparent, and to show how the material would hang when cut in various ways.

It is most helpful to collect a variety of fabrics and to practise designing for them. Handle all types of materials and observe their different characteristics. It is a good exercise to take lengths, drape them on dress stands and with the aid of a few pins try out various effects, then sketch them from the stand.

As an exercise sketch freely—in a sketch pad or on a sheet of paper—details such as hem lines, bows, collars, folds, etc., in a particular material. This will help you, when designing, to convey the feel of the material and its characteristics into your design sketch.

Grain

The designer uses different directions to obtain the effect desired. Material is cut on the cross, when the line normally running along the straight thread is at an angle of 45 degrees. When cut in this way the material will fall in soft folds and drape.

PEN & INK

Study the draping quality
of the different fabrics.

Textures and patterns

You can achieve a number of effects by using pen and ink, crayon, felt pens, brush and paint, watercolours, coloured inks, etc. I have suggested some of the effects you may obtain on the following pages and I have illustrated in different stages the various techniques which have been used. As an exercise practise those illustrated, then work out some of your own, using different media. Remember that it is only necessary to suggest the texture: your sketch would look far too solid and heavy if you were to fill it all in.

Patterns need only be suggested. It is not necessary to reproduce the pattern on your sketch in every detail; simply suggest it on one side of the figure. It is most useful to indicate the cut of the material by showing the pattern on the cross etc.

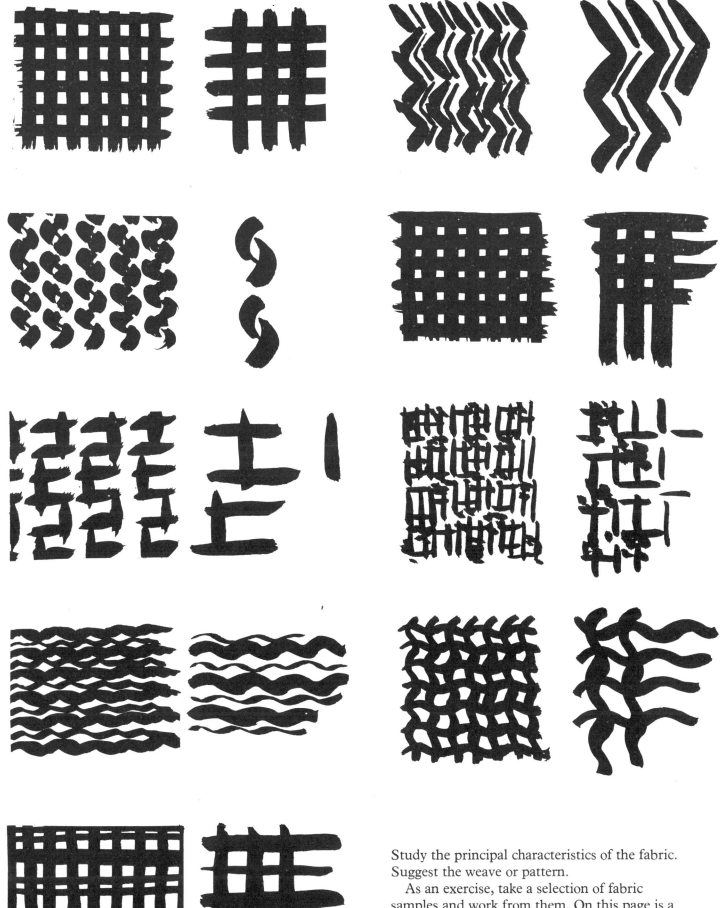

Study the principal characteristics of the fabric. Suggest the weave or pattern.

As an exercise, take a selection of fabric samples and work from them. On this page is a selection of weaves, showing with a few brush strokes how an effect can be achieved.

1

2

3

4

Try the four stages illustrated for a tartan material. Work out your own variations. Remember, these need only be suggested on your sketch to give the effect required. If fabric is cut on the bias this should be indicated.

BRUSH

FIBRE POINT PEN

BRUSH

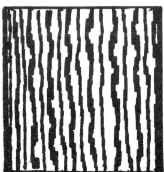

FIBRE POINT PEN

BRUSH

BRUSH

BRUSH

BRUSH

DRY BRUSH

FELT PEN

SILHOUETTES

When considering the silhouette or line of your design
it is most important to be aware of the figure round which
you are designing. Carefully consider the cut of the
bodice, the flare of the skirt, the shape of the sleeves and
the balance of the garment.

When working out ideas and experimenting with shapes,
lines, etc. you may produce many sheets of sketches before
achieving the effect you wish.

As an exercise, sketch a variety of shapes over the same
figure, varying them as much as possible.

Note how a slight variation of line can change the look
of the garment.

Sketch the figure by applying
light pencil lines, then design
your garment over the figure.
Remember that the garment
surrounds the figure and the
fabric will fall according to the
weight, cut, texture, etc.

TECHNIQUES

Materials

Paper: layout pad, packets of blank paper, detail paper, sketch pads, drawing board.

For presentation work it is suggested that you use the following: hand-made paper, pastel paper, tinted paper, fashion boards, sugar paper.

Drawing pins: steel clips to hold drawing paper or pad to board.

Pencils: B and 2B pencils are suggested for sketching. A ballpoint pen is also used for quick sketching. Drawing pencils of various degrees of softness and hardness; H or HB pencils are hard, B or 2B are soft.

Pens: drawing pens; with a selection of pens, nibs can usually be purchased on a card reasonably priced. Fibre-tipped pens with ink refills for drawing. Felt pens in black and other colours. Ballpoint pens with refills. Fountain pens which can be filled with black ink for sketching. Rapidograph pens with a selection of different size nibs; these are more expensive than the other pens listed but they are most useful to produce good work.

Brushes: a selection of good sable brushes size 4, 6, 8. It is worth investing in good brushes.

Colour: a wonderful selection of coloured inks can be easily obtained. Designers' colours should include a wide variety. Water colour box. Colour pencils. Wax crayons.

Care of Brushes: good paint brushes are expensive and you should therefore take great care of them. Brushes should always be washed after use with cold— never warm—water. When used with Indian ink they should be washed with a mild, pure soap and cold water. Dry the brush with a soft cloth and bring to a point. Never allow it to dry with the hairs curved or spread. Always place your brushes in a container, e.g. jam-jars, water pots, etc. resting upright on the handle.

Palettes: for mixing your paints a large, clean palette is essential. Palettes can be obtained from Art shops, or as an alternative, a selection of old saucers or tiles may be used.

Erasers: a good selection of erasers may be obtained from Art shops or Stationery shops. Typewriter erasers are useful to remove heavy black lines in ink.

Stretch Paper: stretch paper is saturated with water, then gently stretched on all sides, placed on a board and taped with gum paper. This is then allowed to dry smooth and taut. It is then ready to work on. Having completed the presentation work cut from the board to the required size. This method would be used only when presenting work which requires a high standard of finish and when washes are used.

Portfolio: a portfolio to keep your work in is essential. Various types can be purchased. However, with the use of some stiff cardboards and tape you can produce one yourself. I suggest that you date your work so that you can compare the progress you are making. It is also a good idea to break down your work according to the designs, i.e. day dresses, coats, suits, evening wear, children's wear, etc. It is always advisable to keep your folder in good order and to be able to refer to the various sections at any time.

The fur effect has been achieved by applying,
very lightly, dry paint.

Brush and pen combined. Experiment
with various techniques by using
different pens to achieve the effect
required. Remember that patterns,
textures, etc. need only be suggested. A
few lines can express all you wish to say
without going into great detail.

These sketches were drafted at a fashion show.
The work was finished off after the show by
applying pen and ink with black wash over candle
wax to achieve velvet effect. The materials were
black velvet and brocade.

Black satin. The effect is achieved with black poster paint applied with brush. Highlights of material are obtained with white paint and finer details with pen and ink.

These three sketches in pen and ink illustrate linen
dresses with top stitching. Notice that the young
look has been achieved by giving the figures youthful
hair-styles and poses and that the figures have been
indicated by a few lines only.

Rapidograph

These black line drawings were done by using a rapidograph pen, giving a perfect flowing line. Take care when indicating the stitching and make sure this is in line and spaced correctly.

1 *Lace:* practise producing a lace effect by carefully studying the pattern
   of the lace and then indicate simply with the use of a few lines the
   pattern on one side of the figure, as illustrated. This effect has been
   achieved with a fine mapping pen.

2 *Beading:* when indicating the beading the pattern need only be
   suggested, emphasizing the main effect of the beads. A fibre-tipped pen
   has been used to obtain this effect.

3 *Appliqué:* when indicating appliqué work remember that you should
   emphasize that the 'appliqué' would be in relief. Notice in the above
   drawing the effect of the appliqué sleeves.

Evening gown in black velvet. Notice the white line indicating seams and panel line. This can be applied with white paint, using a fine brush; or—when painting—leave the white paper to indicate seams, etc.

Ballpoint

Notice the pattern indicated on one side of the figure. When reproducing
a fabric design, make a study of the main pattern and repeat it.

Ballpoint pen has been used for these illustrations. Notice the
subtle changes of waist bands and bodices. When designing
remember to experiment with the design by varying the
proportions, line, etc.

Sketches made from fashion shows. Quick line sketches made with fountain pen and ink taken from my sketch book. When working at fashion shows, making sketches, you should develop a technique enabling you to express quickly the essential line and details.

Pen and ink

Raincoats sketched by using pen and ink. Notice the clean, simple line and details: placing of buttons, the yoke line, belt, etc. No. 2 has been drawn by using brush and black poster paint. Notice that great care has been given to details: seams, pocket, collar, etc.

Brush

2

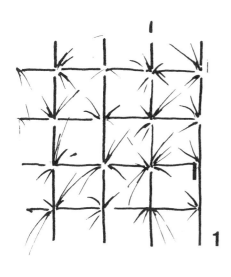

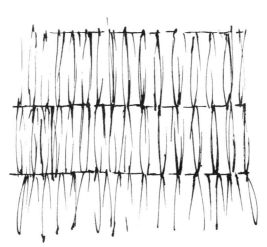

1

2

3

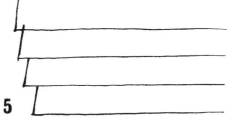

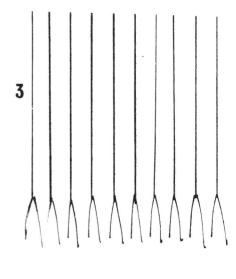

4

5

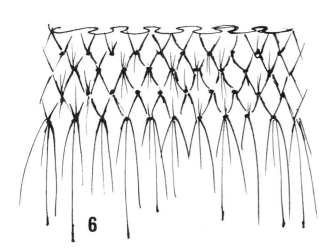

6

7

Illustrating different treatments
of fabrics.

1 Quilting
2 Ruffling
3 Pin Tucks
4 Shirring
5 Tucking
6 Smocking
7 Fringing